T0083814

BLOOD
OBOE

BLOOD
OBOE

DOUGLAS PICCINNINI

OMNIDAWN PUBLISHING
OAKLAND, CALIFORNIA
2015

Cover art by Darren McManus.
Digital Composition for Blood Oboe, 2014.
www.darrenmcmanus.com

Book cover and interior design by Cassandra Smith

Offset printed in the United States
by Edwards Brothers Malloy, Ann Arbor, Michigan
On 55# Heritage Book Cream White Antique
Acid Free Archival Quality Recycled Paper
with Rainbow FSC Certified Colored End Papers

Library of Congress Cataloging-in-Publication Data

Piccinnini, Douglas.
  [Poems. Selections]
  Blood oboe / Douglas Piccinnini.
    pages ; cm
  ISBN 978-1-63243-009-0 (pbk. : alk. paper)
  I. Title.
  PS3616.I234A6 2015
  811'.6--dc23
                        2015017593

Published by Omnidawn Publishing, Oakland, California
www.omnidawn.com   (510) 237-5472   (800) 792-4957
          10 9 8 7 6 5 4 3 2 1
          ISBN: 978-1-63243-009-0

Acknowledgments

I am grateful to the editors of the following publications in which some of the poems in this book first appeared and often in different form. Additionally, some sections previously appeared in the chapbook *Soft* (The Cultural Society, 2010).

Aufgabe
Best American Poetry Blog
Brooklyn Review
Columbia Review
Fawlt Magazine
Lana Turner
Lyre Lyre
Poetry Crush
The Seattle Review
SET
So & So
Vanitas
VLAK
Verse
Well Greased

LIKE WILTED MINT IN PUBLIC REVIVED

BON ENERGY

He has done it—written poems of a gnarled toughness that can't be taken apart, chewed up, seen through. Douglas Piccinnini (the delightful name itself is incongruously dance-like, operatic) has set the mark for new poems of a terrific integrity, unsmiling (their humor is deep down, waiting); poems sharply seeing. Seeing, for instance, that the mathematical universe is maddeningly out of synch with the negative numbers of the daily emotions that cannot catch up with the day: "what's this dumb rope to cling to." Where is the sum? The transcendence? "All the coin towers / tooth down." No one else concentrates so mercilessly on the phenomenology of the existentially shorted day, the not-ever-all, the fractured (where "Symbolic debris stands / in the trees for trees"), except of course Samuel Beckett, whose work Piccinnini's doesn't otherwise resemble, and in a more rarefied atmosphere, Paul Celan. What Celan is to poetry after Auschwitz, Piccinnini is to the crushingly secular rhythm of a false progress ("a fiction moved / from seed / to leave enough room / to land"; "'clear of' then moan / to know to hear the condition"). He has his own sear, even if he, too, writes of blocked or anyway extremely difficult hope in short, acute, alarming uncompromising statements (usually fragments, "broken spokes of [the] carriage") on the negative

9

side of negative theology. Anyway, he's further down the slope, in "Faith Void," bruised by the talus. In one poem he even nods to Celan: "to say the gold milk / of eternity and the blue / milk of eternity are one / not even air I guess hurts," not, that is, if air is as neutral as eternity, where "distance . . . maths the mind," far from "this place, the acreage / as an animal I incorporate." The "condition" of the person who is always on trial, a moaning *nearly* one who doesn't coincide with the neutral *one*, can make said pseudo-one feel aggressive: "Life is 'terrible.' I get hungry: / It's time to punch everyone."

"*[Y]on hope spanks / yon hope steams*" models this poet's remarkable penetration and compression—the compression magnetized to the "one" of the neutral underlying or hovering at the edge of impossible conflict, and the penetration finding that nothing is therefore quite itself, but instead scattered in a vortex of contradictions. Hope spanks like a birth whack, good; is a punishment, bad; a perverse pleasure, good but also bad. And hope *steams* because it is drive and a "system evaporating," a hot breath in the cold, a hot meal, urine hitting snow. To stop there. The six monosyllables are stiff from too much to say. Piccinnini often names to the side, denying easy object-reference and a supposed primary nomination. The word is already false insofar as it presents itself as an adequation. Hence this poet's insistence on writing poems that undergo and desist at the same time, even in single phrases ("Like the smells of. / To the balcony of.") Each short sentence is a determined thing, but close to stoppage. Each little stanza is at once urgent and blocked. Which of course leaves the poem gaping open and impossible to close (never mind that it's all fists and punches). The words themselves are anyway agape—generic, bundling nouns.

Piccinnini needs poetry "to look my sorrow in the face," to quote Aragon. And he needs the prospect of the reader in order to *undergo* thought and avoid "inert ideas / like negative streets."

He drives the words forward, and sometimes his restaurant-kitchen-spawned Spanish interrupts the English (young Piccinnini is a chef) to see how much rubber *it* can burn. ('que malo / que chingo"—quite a lot). His language is tough, as he's tough: "life is a gang. / now get. moisten." Piccinnini is utterly accomplished, but not in the old, easily recognizable ways. He's quick and furious but he never goes wrong, even if his subject is that everything is wrong.

The second of the book's three divisions, "Like Wilted Mint in Public Revived," opens out from "I" and "my" to generalities, "food, rooms, appetite," "the stars / over our garages," the "opaque public" ("who is there / that I shake out a name[?]") And the final section, "Bon Energy," struggles to be brighter ('the fuse deep in the carpet" and "the place," though "missing room [,] still place." So "try not living / after anything the way a hand smells / w honey and clover w glass and saliva"). At moments it is almost tender in its regard for a, or the, "you," "the optimal person." But in *Blood Oboe* these terms, if positive, are relative. They are clipped by "clipped moods." The "twisted route of glad" may go "onward / at the difference beyond," but, well, it's a "blank" hymn, "unprofitable."

Most poetry is quite innocent of what Piccinnini finds staring into his face and slapping it. Poetry this psychologically astute and "metaphysically" wised up and wilted is extremely rare. And this is not even to mention that by comparison with his, most poetry is slack and uninventive. It smashes, in one fell blow, all the current nonsense about the impossibility of originality. Piccinnini is an instant asset to American literature. Consider only that there is no other longish American poem even remotely like "Clean." It's all bare bones—knuckles. Its violence comes at the reader in tight, local spots, but it's still an imaginative violence pressing against the violence of the life world, and its hard-bitten tone and temperament are of a striking kind scarcely foreseen by the great, smooth-talking Wallace Stevens.

TO KNOW TO HEAR THE CONDITION

to proceed and not unlike want

I want to tell you tones

step to tones

in an ahistorical sense

the storied past

mute descant—

my happened variance

drawn shadow

light seed—

in that first banter

the screen rinsed

of its insidious delirium—

in that gift

its fresh arrest

of flattened repose

15

in every segment

the sheet bent

upon its unwashed self

as an observer

to open the reticule

the difficult jar—

what's this area

talked thru blood

between numbers—

enough sun is never

enough sun to numb

the weeks' returns

then the number

when frisked, the numeral

to sound as ever

to eat through every basic day

to yank "clear of" then moan

to know to hear the condition—

farewell particular care

I've bottled to blow to pieces

a few obvious not-beens I've been

the remainder a soft task

a deselected driver pushed against

memory's breakable seine—

what's this dumb rope to cling to

the speech called, verbed over

prevailed, rote symptom

work's toy into grief

an other beat by data

you, inflexible glow

FAITH VOID

NEW FEELING

Like the smells of.
To the balcony of.

Little dream choke. Little
flame. Little triplet kill.

Transdreamed, a state parallel
downs so much pathetic weight.

Give out young chuckle,
my salty excuse.

Yon hope spanks.
Yon hope steams.

FAITH VOID

I to a looser, saprophytic practice
steeped in lost coinage.

It's time I chew
abrupt books to nothing.

Symbolic debris stands
in the trees for trees.

A feel fruits through.
You thought you thought

more about things than
colors do rhyming.

SERVING THE HEAD

Only smooth channeling.
Only soothing annuals
to ear the way.
Which that I see

tingling fury
so possessive following
doubling becoming.

All the states
throat up.

All the coin towers
tooth down.

PLAY

Por love of noon
cracks the grape
feeds the sky
pours its plain young
explaining on everything.

In the thistle I hear
wind coming too

maudlin wind
so full and filling.

NEGATIVE JUICE

what waster of song
drones beyond light

beyond aerosol shadow

the breath I mean pacing in this helmet
the void of force stamped

the "howcanwelivewithout
theunknowninfrontofus" glance
buscando sombre

que malo
que chingo

LONG PIG

Vitrified waves stop the palate

and fix in celluloid clots, I mean
in the winter of poor hygiene
a slate dust sanctifies the glass.

Life is "terrible." I get hungry:
It's time to punch everyone.

CATBRAIN

lo único cosa que hago es esperar
the only pantomime is my focus
the only slangy thing I think of—
meme—I can't think

life is a gang.
now get. moisten.

first the chariot then the race
first the chicken then the salad
so I realize I'm bleeding.

so much wilderkind goes on
itself in boring reform.

"I" sleep. I sleep. Delete.

MOUTHING

an eightish feel I click to
as a tribute a strafe

my property of cells
my "my"
as decharmed
as ever
accordions in

the old golden age of sadness
piece of trash in the wind

blood in the hopper

to say the gold milk
of eternity and the blue
milk of eternity are one
not even air I guess hurts

NUGATORY

mi cuerpo sólo
porque el viento sopla
y sopla

y se insiste en los manos
y la luz se insiste"
and I begin

in incondite sound—
warmth from the ear
as I crawl to some

bottled waking
all grinding to say
what's this key for

youth se puedo
as the sun in extinction
is a fantasy

bring the tongue
for I feel like a drug
but find no scar

no delirium
no sebum released
nor emptied drum at this pace—

rare until I read my dark
is your dark should misery
touch a clock

que llamar el aire
que se ajusta la vela"
force me in a way

for a day that pail
lower inside you, no higher
sad partisan

se ve asintiendo
oblivion
my drained fen

"yo sé que es mojada
y que el sol no brilla"
pero vivimos todavía

as I find my drink
to be a house
too upsetting to the eye

you're not interested.
like an excess—
the flatness

of this prime
an age ago here again
unmended, availed.

the nonce—
what I'd do to you
to not exist. To slip.

what frontier choice-
lessness becomes. There's me
there's you there's me.

Sharp, stiff, bloodless leaf.
I'll know you not through
cause deserved though

understood—surrender.
pour golden or
ring a voltage

to a system evaporating.
Rag the ceiling.
Dubious egress

aiming at a friend
ever to regain consciousness.
Make sure I'm fed.

AS IN EVERY ISM

spread by runners—
poor creeping
for one day hate is

pure stimulation
preceding kink
"simulation"

one way of grieving
a dethroned self
one mouthful of being—

an aeon of inert ideas
like negative streets
the suffocating pill

softening the body
through touch-
less immobility.

NUGATORY

memory itself is not
welcome—a match then
unlit in my pocket

to want to bloom
a grief and give up
this feeling

but grief is
my own number, coming
late, disremembering

COLD DRINK

everyone could touch the rope

the shirt too of youth in this lower sky
the false sirs already dead young
the weakness now cooled

everything titted up—unrhymed

that was the onset of our adorable years

the earth loved us a little I remember"

WILDLIFE

my green is my green"
and trending
and huge

woodlings porch
the ordinary forces

and caked w fur
and seasoned

the water beads
around my leathery beak.

Let's not think about
breaking let's not break
anymore of my things.

ECLOSION

Little mind. Somehow
homeschooled weapons, daddy.
The laziest weapon
greener stallion jogging
con guns in the hall.

Some selected soft tooth soldiering
college dough. "I come out"
to you thru websites.
Websites? Websites.

SOBRE SKIDS

To climb sueños
cotton folding clean pay
the juice box empties.

Cada línea verbs state.
Mi vida. Tu vida. Mi spungled tongue.

I'm into so much worried paint.
I'm training news and the weather
in a big way blows all this
broken sober bad.

EMPTY ZAPATOS

You alone. I'm alone. You're
alone. Slow explosions.
That much I do
with none duende.

Then the colt flew.
Mouth staved air.
The air big air.

I'm glad everything worked out.

LIKE WILTED MINT IN PUBLIC REVIVED

They too wait. If not far.
A road for you, angel. Toward
the opaque public. Reached for.

Leagues of regret. Hence the rook
hunkered. The system sprinkling
down its moved body.

And outward nor I, dusted.
Cleared of milk. Drank calm.
Agate bands weakened. Dawn relaxed.

A note scudded. Its edge the rim
felt as a coach between entries.
And led as far too, for you.

The hill as satisfied. As kept
colorful good and wait. In this
lonesome stoppage, urged along.

Lived in. Appointed slant to kiss
as we go. The athletes wading
in hay piles and rightened.

Enough build to assume. Life
lessness becomes. The shore cleaned.
Its beach even met. Home and open.

The floor. The stove. Back through
a map to fold out area. Top themes.
Weird joys. Embattled alleys.

Not alone. A door. The room
from here and without. Arms.
Fixed gentile. Wide gulf.

Friends of them, snow.
A moveable door into
details. Half pay. The dish

pushed across the hall.
All moon figures shine
banked to pieces.

Mechanically down. Oil
on the part most then.
Blood entrenchment.

Its face a cargo
of conclusion.
O, swell, wash

to cancel a pattern—
that channel I
feel none.

This equipage
that term—the old
cancer of things

moves in prayer moves
and deforms, makes
a brain a victim, begins.

The gold foundation
stanchion arranged
rapidly. Blood recovery.

The key askew
and so slight a return
in tarred retrieval. A tune

sung vaguely. To eye
the bending ear of re-
constitution. What

then, "size," a kind of
destiny. A house, not
my house, "growing."

So the sky moves.
The besom ablaze.
As though the hands

intone opinions, the stars
turning. The stars
over our garages. Our tree

at last capable of feeling.
As an area blooms
imperceptibly. This shoot

to spring nothing
but alone
sour the color.

"LITTLE" "BEAR"

I've said so cover'd and un
"the fruit is real"
the something as much

retain me

who is there
that I shake out a name

a system like the sun
is as arable

so I grow incurably so

entre amigos

woods? si, woods
spring the lock
in that I so nilled
semi-anonymous
like wilted mint
in public revived
I will

ECLOSION

the mainspring of
antennae shifting
salience again

the eyehold is
a testimony
say "I knew someone"

antedate cloud made of cloud
leavening
too *in* a self

the gravid air
heaving unreal
problem of calm.

BOWERY

to freeze and lift why alone
abandoned stream
in season—se vende

fundamentally who you are
verbed until you are
a dead system— a debt

of uncut forest—a head
parts of a street
scene behind a building

gas of interior cinema
in a burning time
a smoking time

in a want unsaid
wish you never—
the note seeded

pinning extremity
washed and well
beyond recognition.

CLEAN

or am I me, like "play"—
a corruptible dust

clotted then flowing
as with ease in air—

the breath in expanse
its own portage

to course not feeling
should a ray instruct

and conclude heart dry
unfettered transfer—

drone on eidolon
which if we begin, the beginning

toward things thinking
if to enter, a gate persists

saying this is the obstacle
knowingly constructed, the

way of telling
the area around the mark

too unlike the mark to be
the mark also, but its teacher

and to recall this occasion
borne across affairs

clothed, moneyed in
food, rooms, appetites.

Setting off, symmetry "to die
for" deception, the cloud seeing

halved, the sound approached
with speed and now, distance

decreased, maths the mind
so points the mind with the mind—

this place, the acreage
as an animal I incorporate.

Wires, glass, the bolt securing
each moment to the next

but its opposite non-bolt
engulfing impulse

where sea charges
in a sick foam

to claim the shores broken stones—
hands, "feelings," organs

growing when the world sleeping
more than I asleep also

prepares for day or evening
its can opening, turning air.

No—enforced goodnights this way
stepping through a look

which is the locked face
glassing my inexpression

a kind of haunting
hums, arranges each hair

vibrates along the neck
to distinguish time in time

however frail and small
a sound to rip through—

and to your mouth come
the story of yrs like woods

with the faces of yrs in them
distorted and still

now lighted with the burning
broken spokes of that carriage.

Could we put down
food, grief, the toy, what

we are chewing
sown into, though I

extend this section of rubber hose
which water has entered

and now section that I hold
near to my eye

as the world is received
that has been growing

and while growing, still
cut by the blade, trimmed

and scored by the blade now dull—
if you could repel

what you are and still would be—
would you be this hide over the barrel

detuned, beat on
with the hands and were you—

once, I would see anything
and flies were the dreaming

and higher up, young branches
there feelings, there things

within the service
the ends of membranes

tails of light, never heard
so touched.

Walking, still waking, the center
closed, each stroke to design

a fiction moved
from seed

to leave enough room
to land

so projected
the pace to reach sound

the teeth as poorly prepared
to speak an outland speech

poor parallel time
to say nothing and offer nothing

from sleep, from sitting and soon
kneeling, no sooner dreaming

we savage and they
inform nothing—

screens upon every drama
small, dram in the mouth

yrs to join up in each
telling sign, the leaves

snapping, the branches
baring the nest

to pose against sky
and we are not sorry

for a tearswept wound
shoveling ash to mouth

the spit dark lips alive
the meal still digesting

nursing a geography
cleansed of conclusion

last we have worn
our face from our face

the nonlook pebbling dark
the organ lameshape

and shovel life against life
to groom the system—

The strongest of all around us
sparks the particle kind

flexes the mast
but mast remains

knife glinting, rising
to fall upon the meat

taking meat from meat
maneuvering tissue

this portage of cells, disfiguring play—
bloodpoor and if only blood

then bones too when said so minor
to be a part of the structure

is to be in service to the structure
to screw you into a corner

the habit diagramming
the sheet revealing

an absence bright
enduring glow.

Increased heaven. Willful smudge.
Inform them, lucky as they are.
A ceiling built into it. I've opened.

Touched a specific spreading.
Not whitened. Knotted.
And zones, not able. Faint, set

deep off the curve. Again
they appeared. Why? Such
blankets and august mouths.

I receives, ground, a swell
washed, a rest of.
About lifts. Favored range.

Less the grammar's remainder.
Here. Our timed something. First
phrased over a better math.

Its exact wreck pulled in.
Weighed press. Smoothed down.
A prefigured meal and delayed pose.

Out of there. Even field.
Its flattened bill. Its black sewer
of replete close.

Or, in exchange. Light
flashing through metal.
A post knocked free.

Jade. Over hours. Its slacked
minute to touch. A sort of storm
verbs the air, to sign.

To elevate in swim. To wait out
the lozenge of spit. Fur
the general cloud fitness.

I mean some (small spout) and taste
article dead, torn each in
pause. Its mini-flag collapse. Then dive

from them, well-bruised.
A sense of material stretching.
That video, a unit of ends.

BON ENERGY

NUGATORY

the "correct" channel in detail
is dust by dust of skin to frame
in one way the "disdain of generations"

apathy ifs to "wake" this scenery—
banners of unapproachable past
nonfruiting flower in the window.

to say I've come up in absurd discharge
a way of not knowing
the particulars of any sound—

I leave my love as yet
as blue is a "color" as black is
"endless" "space"

OLD WEATHER

pressure in the skull
I'm told to end—might
my boat fold

a presage I guess
to slowly winter?
to light where you are?

a habit thinking of you
when it's not now—
that radar becoming

this windowless feel that
nosunnorshaddow
panic of everything

NOT FLOWERS

by surrender
a curfew
to a purpose

to know you
brings air
furs as warm

and whatever I guess
unsilenced, persists
in a draft above

punches to pierce
an unfed cache
of indeterminate deep.

clipped moods. Until
a word to you, devoured answer.
The object soap white. Recoiled

through a day's format. As
it is arrived at in secret. A
dropper of and so vivid.

Sitting like them. Anguished.
Adjusted denial. A bridge
almost high, seduced, explained.

In place of music, blanked hymn.
Its twisted route of glad. Full
time and spirit, rained in.

_____To meet
aching through the pill. Two
or three things to know about them like.

As I, in my own part interested
unprofitable and onward
at the difference beyond.

NO MIEDO COMO EL FUTURO

Sleeping lather. The cool
at thighs being gives
roots earth the way

leaving produces juice.
In an opened balloon the worm
receding. The unzipped

kind fleshing.
I woke this century my beard
dusty the shadow shortened

the air cut to fly in.
But with mint to see if I
remember anyone

sparkling gesture.
Places to go. Places
you go so young

and orange. With reds
with your coat on the floor.
I'm inside and I live here.

No gold only golds
crush the floor.
Crucial floes about

distance as ever
fleet shifting. Think off.
Then thinkless.

A sink burying mouth
with such bright snapping.
Think of it as educational

road darked future. The place
missing room still place.
And this arrested devotion. Though pleas

lard thee. And in artful
arrangements the vertebrae
fix thee so.

Come now come
my burning sugar
my burnt grain

my smoking door.
Give out yon tender dreamstuff.
Dram consciousness.

Willow brushes
for the lake. Go on and not
expelling. Try not living

after anything the way a hand smells
w honey and clover w glass and saliva
for sullen thunder

clouds east.
So distant honey. Near honey.
For lost time. For sweet use.

Pour vous torn carpel
the bell kind.
Besos.

Bon sleep. Bon energy. So textures
confer in healthy notes.
Saws empty as light. The fuse

deep in the carpet.
And instruments of—
your we out of tongue so I

keep learning broken pottery.
Limn that transdreamed field
one arching feeling

ship of.
No bottom to the ether
nor air basket w gloves for it

w husks nor the meat
w my green over it
w whatever isn't there too

single terrifying smell.
This small shelter of blue
in black. Now go.

Dumbly driven in
by the lateness in time
as if time weren't moving

with itself so stilled
or hand to beard or breast
brings this capsule down

and a red thought through blues
a break in the age
the humors unmoved.

VALERIAN

inch except not in silence
I mean to be crippled if anything
smeared in a dream

to sleep by "breathing" in
a closing logic
to view your body

above your body
a perhaps love like
hanging awareness

chill to quote you
rending sheet
of fermentation—

my agony by yours
a greening branch
and maybe lack of sky

A hornet climbs the air. Gold fuse.
Closet of crutches. Branches torn
by the storm. Down stiff gutter.

Roosters as they were. At home.
Chimes bring sun. The ground
with light, averaged gravity.

The controlled kind, toward calm.
Ivory studded with iron. Pulp.
The air as sweet. Bright flower.

My pores open. Common someone.
Hotels. Pools. Banquets. Cold trays of fish.
Depictions of. Balsa. Pine. Cherry.

Announcements. A test grammar into pointing.
Coasts appear wrung with garlands.
This liquor in verbatim. Colorful stone.

Wafers upon the lake ice. Thinking
to then. Children's voices. A flood
between the blossom time and fruit.

JOSEF KAPLAN

'til fully in weights,
si, my most feeling sheeted
this minor tribe right quick

so my nth sweet is like ya
a big sweety in my sights
sorta batteried out and sleepy

sorta coning around a necrotext
everything and my pet
backing into everything

in labor to stay with my my-
thology to stop crying some color
and dialogue güey—

everybody knows a trenchcoat
in absentia in the wind
unbroken ovum for a seed jar

if an ulcer then none—
nonverbal spectrum
the "I don't want that"

tongued DAD mug
to smash you like "like"
no puedo a hacer esto

para que sea especial
no, let's do this, hey,
champ I'm tired

feeding the garland
afraid of my son
in some curtaining nonplace

Carriage, its own distant conclusion.
And the optimal person, not auto
sped neighborhood.

Have beens. The voice
fed fumes, a real middle.
About then and flushed. Spilt

innocence. A western
course sighing. Novel slips.
As you asked, none.

Born, sampled, pardon
ed. You however beau.
Sorted, tame enough.

A rope of cough.
Not climbing some
single pleasure. Its in

habitants. The surface
sealed, darkly. Its absorbed
orbit to stand under.

At term to peace. The farm. The limbs
curled in. Not more to resume beyond
the take. So to saw through waves.

With, at present, the cure. Able. Freed.
Approached as the hub to continue
wheeling about or, as curious

to see that escaped value and minus.
Some immanent broom to crystal out
the cloud's perceived malice.

Land then. Uniformly broken. At rate
collected and birthed away. From you
comes again. The same I meet.

News. Ashes. The most vacuum.
Parted to orchard and join. Collected
as fooled diagrams of fear. Juiced.

But back then. Returning each
minute to itself. A plan shed from
its marble arches. And blood oboe.

Photo Credit: Brandon M. Jones

Douglas Piccinnini was born in New York City in 1982. His writing has appeared in *Antioch Review*, *Aufgabe*, *Diner Journal*, *Jacket*, Lana Turner, *The Volta*, *Verse*, *The Poetry Project Newsletter*, NYTimes.com and *The Seattle Review*—among other publications.

He has been awarded residencies by The Vermont Studio Center, Art Farm in Marquette, NE and, The Elizabeth Bishop Society of Nova Scotia. In 2014, he was selected by Dorothea Lasky as a winner of the Summer Literary Seminars for Poetry.

Piccinnini is the author of several chapbooks including *Soft* (The Cultural Society) and *Flag* (Well Greased Press)—an encoded chromaglyph. *Story Book*, a novella, is forthcoming with The Cultural Society.

Blood Oboe
by Douglas Piccinnini

Cover and interior text set in Avenir LT Std.

Cover art by Darren McManus.
Digital Composition for Blood Oboe, 2014.
www.darrenmcmanus.com

Cover and interior design by Cassandra Smith

Offset printed in the United States
by Edwards Brothers Malloy, Ann Arbor, Michigan
On 55# Heritage Book Cream White Antique
Acid Free Archival Quality Recycled Paper
with Rainbow FSC Certified Colored End Papers

Publication of this book was made possible in part by gifts from:
Robin & Curt Caton
Deborah Klang Smith
John Gravendyk
Barbara White, Trustee, Leaves of Grass Fund

Omnidawn Publishing
Oakland, California
2015

Rusty Morrison & Ken Keegan, senior editors & co-publishers
Gillian Olivia Blythe Hamel, managing editor
Cassandra Smith, poetry editor & book designer
Peter Burghardt, poetry editor & book designer
Melissa Burke, poetry editor & marketing manager
Sharon Zetter, poetry editor, book designer, & grant writer
Liza Flum, poetry editor
RJ Ingram, poetry editor
Juliana Paslay, fiction editor
Gail Aronson, fiction editor
Josie Gallup, publicity assistant
Sheila Sumner, publicity assistant
Kevin Peters, warehouse manager
Janelle Bonifacio, office assistant
Abbigail Baldys, administrative assistant